THINKING REMOTE

Thinking Remote: Inspiration for Leaders of Distributed Teams
© Pilar Orti and Maya Middlemiss, 2019

Pilar Orti and Maya Middlemiss are hereby identified as the authors of this work in accordance with section 77 of the Copyright, Designs and Patents Act 1988.

ISBN 978-0-9572802-3-6

British Library Cataloguing-in-Publication data

A catalogue record for this book is available from the British Library

Cover design: Manuel Barrio

Design: Simon Hartshorne

Pilar Orti and Maya Middlemiss

THINKING REMOTE

Inspiration for Leaders of Distributed Teams

Contents

INTRODUCTION

Welcome to the world of *Virtual Not Distant*, where we believe that people can work and create together without sharing the same four walls. Sometimes organisations struggle with helping their people transition to an 'office-optional' approach, but with the right mindset it is possible to adopt remote work practices which can enable team members to work together while being apart.

At *Virtual Not Distant* we are immersed in the world of digital collaboration, remote leadership and online teamwork – and we regularly share what we are learning from, and what we are working and reflecting on. We know that remote collaboration is possible, but it involves a different approach to that we have been used to taking in the colocated space. Every month we create in-depth written content, reflecting on specific aspects of remote working and virtual teams – in particular the change management process involved in transitioning from a 'traditional', colocated office setting to something more flexible.

Much of this reflection and discussion goes on in the *21st Century Work Life* podcast, but also we have been populating our blog since the company was set up in 2016. With the aim of sharpening up our message and finding a new set of readers, we compiled a series of blog posts and turned them into this book.

In *Thinking Remote*, we reflect on specific topics and learning points which come out of the current sociological shift. Some of the topics might be high on your agenda, if you are looking at more 'office-optional' possibilities for your team, while others you might not have thought about yet.

We have curated them here, with a set of reflections at the end of each chapter aimed at team leaders and managers. Some of these are designed to be discussed with your team, as part of your ongoing strategy and team-building activities, while others might be more appropriate for internal reflection in the first instance. Every team and every team leader are different, and so will take different things from what follows.

Furthermore, this short book is a handy tool for informal learning within management teams, and readers are encouraged to share and discuss their responses to the leadership reflection questions which are found at the conclusion of each chapter.

We hope this book will be a good starting point for your own journey into the future of work, and in creating systems and culture which help you to get the most out of your own activities and environment.

Pilar Orti and Maya Middlemiss

PART 1

LAYING THE FOUNDATIONS FOR REMOTE TEAMWORK

1. DESIGNING THE DIGITAL WORKSPACE: WHAT WE CAN LEARN FROM THE PHYSICAL SPACE

In this chapter, Pilar reflects on how we can consciously shape our digital workspaces in the same way as our physical ones, and how both environments impact on the culture that we want to nurture and create.

As we learn more about what helps people to be productive at work and the kind of environments that enable collaboration, companies are investing heavily in the design of their physical workspaces. However, the conversation about the digital tools used for productivity and collaboration rarely goes beyond: "Which one shall we use?"

I have observed that little thought goes into designing the digital workspace in a way that is in line with the organisation's or team's culture, or that helps us change it when we need to do so. And often, how little thought is given to how employees will interact emotionally with the space, or how it might encourage spontaneous interaction between people.

The conversation around what makes an ideal office design is getting interesting, so why don't we listen in and apply what we are learning to design the digital workspace better? And while we are at it, let's remember that even in companies not 'going remote', people are still getting most of their work done through technology – so this conversation is relevant to most organisations, regardless of whether they are adopting an 'office-optional' approach.

The physical workspace

In March 2018 I attended an event in London called 'Experimenting with Workspace'. In the session, we looked at how the layout of an office space influences where we sit with others to work on a task together.

We considered how we can design workspaces to encourage certain interactions, and how workplace design can affect them. Often, we need spaces where people can have impromptu conversations in the open, but also where private conversations or work in isolation can be carried out.

For example, one way of encouraging people from different departments to interact is to have only one set of toilets on each floor: to go to the toilet, you need to walk by quite a number of people whom otherwise you might never come across.

This is a very practical solution, and one which can't (yet) be transferred to the digital space. However, the concepts behind it spark some questions to ask ourselves when making decisions about what our workspaces – physical and digital – could look like.

The importance of culture

What is the culture like in your organisation? Is it collaborative or competitive?

If it's competitive, designing an open space for discussion, where everyone can hear everyone else and see each other's designs or scribbles, might not be the best option – that is, unless you want to challenge and change that culture through changing the environment.

The same thought needs to go into designing our digital workspace. If we want to encourage collaboration, we can set up online tools and processes through which everyone makes their work visible to everyone else. However, if we are really competitive, those spaces might end up being unhealthy, bragging noticeboards. Or if we are used to keeping our heads down and barely interacting with anyone else, when we move to online communication, we could end up with an unused space that screams: 'Nobody cares!'

What behaviours are you nurturing?

When introducing any kind of tool, we need to consider what behaviours they are likely to result in, and would like to encourage.

For example, if we want to encourage more transparency in an organisation that is unused to sharing progress and having open conversations, perhaps we can start by encouraging different levels of sharing the work: such as in smaller groups in a team space as opposed to an organisation-wide space, or else in a private group or channel.

....

A team I recently worked with wanted to start 'working out loud' in the organisation – consciously making our work and thought process visible to one another, deliberately putting our work and ideas 'out there' for our team members to see – but they were not used to having conversations in the online, written space.

Their first step towards being more visible in an organisation was to practise sharing their learning, achievements and progress inside the team, before moving on to make their thoughts available to everyone else.

....

If we aren't used to sharing information on a collaboration platform, we might start by facilitating a greater flow of information in live, synchronous conversations when we have more control over who we share information with (mainly, whoever is there), and where we don't end up with a permanent record that results from communicating in writing.

If we want more collaboration, we can start by asking for visibility of the work at a more superficial level (for example, task-level, event-level), then gradually build our 'narration' of the work to sharing the thinking and decision-making processes and wider pieces of work. Or we might decide that our competitive culture is just what drives our business forward, so we avoid setting up systems that are going to dampen that sharp edge.

In any case, give consideration to the kind of space you are building and whether it fits your culture, or whether it's going to help you to shift it to a more desirable one. As you can see, what can help a company grow in the right direction could have a negative effect in another.

Identity and a sense of belonging

One highly-specific function of a building is to separate the organisation from the outside world. When you enter a building as an employee, you know you belong to that place, and usually you know what role you are playing in it.

When designing the digital workspace, we need to be thinking about that as well. Often, this is reflected in the way that intranets are designed. Intranets are not just customised to follow brand guidelines, but also to signal to employees that they are now 'in company property'.

At the team level, you can see this customisation in applications and online tools: in the way that folders are named, how they are organised, the background of project management boards, etc.

So, especially if you are transitioning or putting a team ecosystem together for the first time, ask yourself:

- How do we want people to feel when they enter the digital space?
- What can we do to remind them of where and who they are in relation to that space?

Something as simple as changing the background on a project board, or having a prominent image that is not the company logo, might create a greater sense of connection with the team. It really depends on where you want the locus of engagement to be (that is, what employees connect with, and feel attached to, in an organisation). Again, ask yourself:

- Do we think people benefit from feeling like they belong to the team?
- Do we prefer to remind them that they belong to the wider organisation?

First impressions

When designing a new office layout, a lot of thought goes into what people first see when they enter the space, and what it prompts them to do.

At a simple level, the reception area is usually the first thing you encounter when you enter a building. That makes sense, because it's what visitors are usually looking for, and no one wants them to get lost. But you could make the decision instead to have a prominent staff picture, or a monitor with examples of the company's work, or one that displays a news channel, reflecting how important it is to stay up-to-date with what is going on in the world.

Thinking along the same lines: what do you want your people to do, or even to think, when they log on to the digital workspace?

Here's an example that I came across on the Happy Melly podcast:[1]

Zappos, the online shoe and clothing store, reminds its employees every day of the importance of being familiar with other employees in the company. When an employee logs onto their system at the beginning of the day, a picture of another person in the company pops up with the question, "Do you know who this person is?", and five names from which to choose.

If the employee doesn't pick the right answer, the system tells them their colleague's name and redirects them to that person's profile, so that they can learn a little bit about them.

Zappos is not a remote organisation. However, it is seeing the company grow and is deliberately fostering that sense of connection by making the most out of technology.

This is a prime example of the need to pay attention to the digital space, even when your people are in the same building.

Going back to the collaboration areas in the digital workspace, how you label them will encourage different kinds of behaviours and influence people's relationship with the space. So it is worth giving some thought to how you name the groups, channels, boards, lists and so on – all those areas that make up a collaboration space.

As the lines between physical and digital workspaces continue to blur and merge, we can use aspects from each environment to inform the evolution of the other – until it all becomes just 'work'.

Do we need to keep people together or apart?

How we answer the following questions will depend on the nature of the work, and the size of the organisation or team. In an office:

- Will teams benefit from having all their members together?
- Will they benefit from individuals being able to move around the building, working independently and having access to members of other teams?

---

1   Happy Melly (2017) 'Zappos lives its culture', podcast, 10 November. Available at: www.happymelly.com/zappos-lives-its-culture

Along the same lines:

- Do we need an online space where people can mingle?
- Do we need spaces that belong only to a team, or even to a sub-team?
- Do we need private spaces for individuals which are still online as part of our ecosystem, but where the content only belongs to one person?

Not always together, or not always apart

In most organisations – and even at the team level – there will be examples when you need to provide spaces where people can gather together, and where they can be on their own. Think about an office space: people might have their own desk. There is no reason why, in the digital space, you cannot provide them with a private space too.

First, let's consider the kind of design that encourages interaction between people. I like the concept of the coffee machine in a physical space as an 'attractor' – a spot that draws people to it.

Thinking of the digital space:

- Can you create a space online to act as an 'attractor'? A place where people don't necessarily go to interact with others, but where they might bump into them. For example, a section in your collaboration platform which holds the most recent news or updates.
- Or somewhere that changes its design in a playful way every day, or even a few times during the day?
- Or a platform where people go to when they need to have a chat with someone else?

Key to this kind of attractor is having the functionality to allow you to interact with someone else. It isn't enough to have somewhere that people want to check out often: they need to be able to interact with others when they bump into them there as well.

Now, during the workspace design event I referred to earlier, there was mention of the photocopier machine as being a place where people go to do a specific activity and bump into others. When you think about it, there *are* places like that in the digital workspace. Follow me!

Serendipity in the digital workspace

The immediate place that comes to mind as somewhere that people encounter each other is Google Docs. These are shareable documents such as text, spreadsheets and slide-decks that live in the cloud (other software companies have similar products too).

When you are working on a Google Doc and someone else logs on to it, you can see their avatar at the top of the document.

....

I have often seen Maya in the *Virtual Not Distant* ecosystem, and started to converse within the document itself.

It made me happy to feel that she was there, logged into the same online space at the same time as me – and if I needed something quick from her, all I need to do was click on 'Chat'.

This is a prime example of serendipity in the digital workplace – but it can only happen if we agree to have tools in our ecosystem which have these features. Another place where I have noticed people popping up is in Trello. For example, I was working on a card the other day in preparation for a podcast, and *wham!* – my co-host's profile picture popped up.

....

Finally, one simple feature that makes me feel like I am running into someone in the workspace, is on a collaboration platform or in a chat environment, and the words 'is typing...' appear.

Is there value in serendipitous interaction, and if so, why is it so valuable? For me, in the digital workspace, it gives a sense of connection, of belonging. All of a sudden, it is not just interacting with a document or an app; it is sharing the space with another person – you can envision your colleague at the other end, on their computer. Plus on a practical note, if you need to ask them a quick question, that is the moment while you've got them there.

Caveat: if you are new to working in this way, it might be worth having some sort of conversation about what to do when encountering others online: whether it's OK to hop on a call straightaway, because we know the other person is working on something similar; or whether we need to ask permission first to double check that they can take the call; or whether, actually, we rarely want to be disturbed.

Carefully crafting your digital workspace

As we have seen, we need to put as much thought into designing our digital environment as we do for our physical one. And even when designing the physical environment to introduce smarter, mobile, agile or even activity-based working, we need to make sure that our digital space supports what we are trying to achieve in the physical space. We need to think about them as one.

If you are a completely remote team, there are plenty of things you need to take into account beyond what helps productivity, when deciding on the tools to support your collaboration efforts. I can hear some of you say, "That's all very well, but I'm stuck with a closed system and I can't introduce any of the tools you mentioned." In those cases, review whether your ecosystem is currently working in the way you want it to; if it isn't, figure out why, and whether there is anything you can change in the way that you use it.

If there is no flexibility in how you technically use the tool, could a change in behaviour make the difference instead? For example, if you are using a collaboration tool which doesn't allow you to see that others are working there at the same time, perhaps you can agree to work on the same tasks at given times of the day or week with teammates, to generate that sense of connection.

Or if you cannot customise your team's space to strengthen their identity, what rituals can you introduce into your meetings that will help people feel part of that specific team?

Next steps

Here are some questions to get you thinking about how you are currently using your technology.

- What is your culture like: is it competitive, collaborative or something in-between?
- What is the use of the space encouraging?

- How can you make the digital space unique to your organisation or team?
- Do you have spaces where people can feel connected to each other, and spaces where they can feel they have sole ownership of their work?
- Do you have places where people can meet and feel connected to other people through the work?

If you are not happy with any of the answers to these questions, talk to your team members to see whether this is something that they too would like to change. Review your tools, processes and behaviours, and find one small thing that you can change straightaway.

Leadership reflections

This chapter provokes many avenues for reflection, whether we are working in the same physical space or not. In addition to the questions Pilar leaves you with above, have a think about the following and discuss them with your team.

1. Are we ready to answer these questions about our culture, about what makes our people connect and collaborate effectively? Because if we are 'not there' yet, it might be better to address our team cultural issues before attempting a major transition in how we work together.

2. Does the extent to which we have planned our digital space reflect value judgements in how we think about remote work, or remote colleagues in a hybrid team? If it reflects lack of thought rather than lack of value, how could this be perceived – for example, by someone joining our team as a new remote colleague?

3. Is our digital space congruent with the physical one (if we ever had one), and with our brand values and general appearance in the world?

2. "THOSE TOOLS ARE SO LAST YEAR..."

Delving into the technology that enables us to work online, in this chapter Pilar looks at the extent to which we plan our online work around apps and tools, and how there can be a tendency for 'the tail to wag the dog'. She examines when we should be thinking in terms of what we need a tool to do, then how to find the best solution.

At the time of writing, I am also working on a book on running online meetings. One of the dilemmas (although 'dilemma' might be too strong a word) I am having is how much to refer to current technology. Naming tools and platforms popular right now might well date the book very quickly.

In around 20 years of reading management and leadership books, I have never seen a topic evolve faster than leading technology-enabled teams. The early 2000s saw a range of very comprehensive, high-quality books being published on the subject, but a lot of them are now out of date. Looking for inspiration, I came across a perfect example of this, and thought I would share it with you.

Evolving at the speed of light

I was reading Harvard Business Press's *Leading Virtual Teams* (in the Pocket Mentor series, published in 2010). Most of the material is still relevant today, as it addresses topics such as trust and team identity.

However, only seven years later, the chapter on technology will seem out of date for those of us who have been in the virtual working/collaboration space for a while, although the section on email is still highly relevant!

After considering the benefits of video conferencing, the authors write:

'However, video conferencing can be complicated and costly, only a limited number can participate meaningfully and it typically requires the help of people with technical skills. [...] Unfortunately, systems from different vendors aren't always compatible with different computers. So if your team opts for video, be sure everyone gets a compatible system.'

I must admit that as I share these words with you, I am noticing that even though the first few words seem out of date, the rest of the advice still stands. Everyone on a call or meeting needs to know how to use the technology, and we have to make sure that everyone has access to the right equipment to make the meeting work.

So, totally out of date on one affordability and complexity aspect, but still on-point on the other.

Any tool will do

If this first example made you smile, this second one will widen it. I turned to the section 'Tools for Leading Virtual Teams' and found a series of tables: 'Contact Information for Virtual Team Members', one with a series of questions about the purpose of virtual teams, another table was a 'Culture Check'. Definitely not what I would expect in the section 'Tools for Leading Virtual Teams' only seven years after the book was written.

Although the main reason why I am sharing this with you is in the hope that it will amuse you, it is also a reminder that technology is there to *support* your team's work.

It doesn't matter what the tool is.

What is important is what the tool is *doing for* your team.

The tool might be incredibly simple (for example, a spreadsheet with your team member's location and contact details), or it might be high-end and sophisticated. That is not the point. What *is* important is what the tool *enables you to do*.

Tools are a means to an end

I was working in a virtual team. Although everyone was highly collaborative by nature, some of the team members had never worked in this way before. We were working on a risk assessment, trying to advance the exercise asynchronously in-between our weekly meetings.

I was becoming a little bit frustrated (only a little bit, they were a nice bunch!), and mentioned that we needed to move the work in-between meetings, otherwise the exercise was never going to get done.

"That's easy to say," said Sally, one of the team members, "but the other day I struggled for 20 minutes trying to figure out how to add my suggested mitigation strategies to the tool. I've written them all down, but I haven't figured out how to put them up. Look!"

Then she showed us her list of ideas, written out in her notebook. This made me see how the tool was getting in the way. Not only is it frustrating when we don't know how to use a tool, but Sally had actually lost sight of what she was trying to do. The aim of the exercise was not to use the collaboration platform flawlessly, but to share our thoughts about how to mitigate the risks.

A quick way of doing that – to avoid wrestling for so long – would have been for Sally to upload a photo of her notebook, then ping someone in the team to schedule a separate time to learn how to use the tool.

In that way, we would have had access to her thoughts around the risk assessment so that when we came together in the meeting, we could go straight into the discussion. (And she would have saved herself some valuable time.)

Whether you are excited by a new tool on the market, or struggling to get the new technology to work, remember not to lose sight of what you are trying to do.

Leadership reflections

It's important to regularly review the tools we use to work remotely. These questions are worth examining with your team from time-to-time to ensure alignment.

1. Did we choose the right tool for the job, or the right job for the tool? How

much of our workflow and daily activity is dictated by the thing we use to do it? When did we last review our needs, starting from the most strategic level – a systems-specification level? This could be part of an annual reflection, to develop a brief to scan for anything game-changing which will enable better productivity and performance.

2. 'What do we need to work out loud effectively, with the kind of activities presently occupying the bulk of our output', rather than: 'Is there anything better than Trello now that we should be looking at instead?'

3. Conversely, if you tend to flit from tool-to-tool, continually distracted by the next shiny thing, ask: are we properly assessing the opportunity cost and friction of this switching, including the inevitable learning curve of adoption?

For a marginal gain or a few new features, might it not be better to stick with what everyone knows and really works?

3. THE DANGERS OF 'WORKING OUT LOUD'

We talk a lot about 'working out loud' at Virtual Not Distant. While this is a practice that helps team members stay connected and aligned, we need to be aware of potential pitfalls and the impact that it can have on independent productivity.

In this chapter, Pilar covers the subject from a manager's point of view, while in the next chapter, Maya steps into the shoes of the team member.

Is too much information making us overdependent on each other and destroying autonomous decision-making? As an increasing number of us rely on online tools to check in with our colleagues, unexpected challenges begin to emerge.

Communication underpins all teamwork. The exchange of ideas, information and progress between team members helps people understand how their work affects others, and where (or whom) to go to for help when they need it. At the same time, informal communication helps us take care of our social needs, and to understand others' values and motivations.

Indeed, Sandy Pentland and his team at MIT[2] concluded a few years ago that approximately 30% of a team's variation in performance can be attributed to the patterns of face-to-face communication within the team and with other teams. The important bit here is the patterns: who is talking to whom, not the content.

It is difficult enough to foster high-quality communication when team members share the same physical space (that is, when they are colocated). I have a friend who wanted to organise a team-building day because, in his words, "nobody talks to each other in the office: everyone just stares at their screens". Whether a one-off session would be the answer to this is quite another matter, but the point is, the problem was obvious – lack of communication does not just happen in remote teams.

---

2   Virtual Not Distant (2014) 'WP03: Informal communication in teams', podcast, 27 November. Available at: http://virtualnotdistant.com/informal-communication-in-teams/

Argh... I can't see you!

When we begin to work in a virtual or partly remote fashion, one of our fears is that our communication with team members will be sparse, we will not know what everyone is working on, or we will lose the human connection.

The solution that myself and other 'virtual experts' offer is to 'narrate' your work: to work out loud. So we go into our collaboration platforms every day (be it Slack, BaseCamp, Trello, Microsoft Teams, or any others that might pop up in the next few years), and have visible conversations with team members to avoid losing all the bits of information that we would overhear in the office. We hyper-communicate for fear of under-communicating, and to make sure that we do not lose that sense of 'team'. We communicate openly online, all the time.

This includes you, the manager. Now you can see the conversations that people have about a task. You can read every small request for information or help. You can watch people struggle through their process – one that is essential to them, as they figure out how to innovate. And all the while, because we are trying to move away from the dysfunctional hierarchical structures we all love to hate, you are trying not to interfere.

You are reminding yourself that team members like autonomy, that you don't have all the answers, that you are just creating the environment within which they can thrive. And yet, look at all the information you have about their work progress – there online for you to see, 24 hours a day!

Is giving up control becoming increasingly difficult?

Allow me to share a story from one of my favourite books, *Team of Teams*.[3] The author, General Stanley McChrystal, advocates for flatter, networked organisations and more autonomous decision-making. What I really enjoyed in the book is the use of historical examples of military commanders, who were much less of a control freak than many leaders we might think of today.

Comparing 1860s navy commander Commodore Perry, who was separated from his fleet by large expanses of water, and army official Ulysses S. Grant, who could get his message to his men relatively fast, McChrystal

---

3   Stanley McChrystal with Tantum Collins, David Silverman and Chris Fussell (2015) *Team of Teams: New Rules of Engagement for a Complex World*, Penguin (Kindle edition).

explains: "The inability to communicate with a far-off fleet demanded that Perry be given levels of autonomy he would never have realised as a commander of land forces".

Fast forward to today, when organisational leaders and managers (and actually, all of us) have so much access to what others are doing: "When they can *see* what's going on, leaders understandably want to *control* what's going on".

It's a difficult one. One of our biggest fears is that managers and others in charge of teams struggle with feeling like they have less control over what people are doing, when they are not in the office with them.

So, as we try not to feed that fear by regularly sharing our progress and even our thought process, aren't we just feeding the control-beast instead?

How much information is too much?

So far, we have the tools to stay in touch and keep track of our progress as a team. We have identified the processes which can help us to use the tools effectively, and we are adopting some of the new behaviours for working in this way. Now it's time to start asking ourselves:

- How much information is too much?
- What decisions can I take on my own, without having to run them by team members? (In a colocated space it's very difficult to ask *everyone*, but now it takes as much effort to send a private message as it takes to post it in a team space.)
- Where is the line between offering help and interfering?

In the spirit of teamwork and establishing open communication channels, are we slowly approaching a dangerous dependency on others to do our work? Hopefully not, as long as we continue to review how we work together, establish boundaries and turn off those pesky notifications.

Leadership reflections

If this chapter has given you pause for thought about your own control needs as a leader, or potential overdependencies in your team, here are some ideas to help you surface these consciously for discussion.

1. Is everyone clear about decision-making boundaries, and on what they do and do not need to consult?

Maybe this is explicit in a team agreement, but sometimes it can come about via culture and practice. For example: "If everyone else checks in about refunding small amounts to dissatisfied customers, then I had better run it past my manager too..."

Agreeing as a team about specific operational parameters – for example, "Do whatever it takes to make the customer happy, if it costs less than £50" – is a useful exercise for your team anyway.

2. Am I as a leader projecting any innate insecurities or control-freak tendencies which could be undermining the autonomy of my team members, and making them feel that they have to run everything by me?

3. Is there any tendency for people to 'over-narrate' out of a sense of their own insecurities about visibility?

If so, try reading and discussing the next chapter to consciously surface any underlying presenteeism – either as part of individual performance reviews, or as a team-building strategic direction.

4. NOW THAT I'M REMOTE, CAN ANYONE SEE HOW HARD I'M WORKING?

What can managers of remote teams do to discourage team members from playing the 'presenteeism' game, or using 'working out loud' to show how hard they work, rather than to make the work visible in a way that is useful to others? In this chapter, Maya suggests some ways to nip this behaviour in the bud and avoid its damaging impact on the culture within the team.

In the previous chapter, we discussed the perceived challenge for managers of virtual teams of knowing that the work is getting done. But there is a counterpoint to this situation for the worker being managed – particularly if they are new to remote working. In a former role they will have showed up at a physical workplace, sat at a desk in view of colleagues and participated in face-to-face interactions, from water-cooler banter to formal meetings. It was abundantly clear that they were working hard every day. Frowning at a monitor or banging furiously on a keyboard, closing a deal on a challenging phone call, or staying late to finish an urgent report – all the signs of a diligent employee doing their thing, and making a visible and overt contribution.

But if that team member suddenly finds themselves sitting at home, who is going to see that going on? Especially if they are working on a lengthy project without visible milestones and outputs to feed back on formally. Most of us aren't used to sharing our successes out loud as a matter of course.

Getting noticed versus being productive

This needs thinking about, particularly when transitioning a team to remote working. How are people in the colocated workplace noticed for their productivity? Is there an emphasis on the wrong things, such as presenteeism and long hours?

In the knowledge-worker economy, it can be challenging to measure effectiveness and contribution anyway, even if you are standing over somebody's desk. For example, when hiring a writer, it is not helpful or meaningful to value them by the number of words written, if those words are nonsense and misrepresent the organisation. This is why agreement on the goals and outputs against which the work will be evaluated is so critical – and this really is no different, wherever your direct reports are located.

If you are managing someone who suddenly cannot see you, it can create feelings of vulnerability. For example:

- How will they know that you are aware of how hard they're working?
- What metrics will be used to evaluate their success, or otherwise, in their role?
- How do they know that you know they are not goofing off, watching daytime TV in pyjamas, but still being the same productive team member they always were?

Easing the transition, and helping team members reshape mindset

As a manager you can set expectations, create systems and provide support to enable your colleagues to shift painlessly to effective remote working – which is good for them, for you and for the organisation.

Mindset
Start with your own, and an honest examination of it. It is important to be sure that accountability concerns aren't simply a projection of your insecurities about the new set-up. Any ambivalence about how you will manage their work effectively from a different location is going to show, so make sure you resolve any of your own issues with managing remote productivity first, before you project them onto your team.

Accountability
Be very clear about the degree of accountability and 'working out loud' you expect from your newly-remote team member.

- Are there specific core hours during which you expect them to be contactable and working, or is the work more results-oriented?

- Do you expect them to let you know they are popping down to the post office for 20 minutes, or only diarise if they are likely to be uncontactable for an extended period?

Being clear about fixed calendar points, such as meetings, will help to stop people thinking they need to raise their hand whenever they leave their homeworking desk to go to the bathroom.

You may need to revisit specifics around how their performance will be evaluated, and structure accountability tools toward those indicators. The way you measure this in the colocated space may transfer seamlessly to remote, or it may need some tweaking. Also bear in mind that other than in very specific professions, this rarely relates to anything about time spent on particular activities.

....

I can recall consulting in a client service-based office once, where it emerged that all timesheets were hurriedly reconstructed most Friday afternoons, when HR sent the reminder email out – and constituted little more than creative guesswork in most cases as a result.

So, that wasn't working.

....

"Look at me and how hard I'm working!"

It's important to nip in the bud any demonstrated tendencies to replicate 'presenteeism' games in the online office. Replacing the 'jacket on the back of the chair' with a habit of checking out shared documents ridiculously early in the morning, or replying to emails and instant messages late at night, shouldn't impress anyone. From a supervisory point of view, all it points to is poor time management skills in need of remedy.

Similarly, be ready to constructively challenge any emergent culture of martyrdom, where team members might feel the need to boast about their all-nighters, or play games of long-hours one-upmanship. How many hours each person needs in order to deliver their work is an individual performance management issue, and if this starts to become a public yardstick for success, there is something very unhealthy going on in the team.

Remember that remote working can greatly improve productivity and focus, especially on deep work tasks. So, make sure your team members know that it's actually fine if they get things done more quickly and efficiently than they did in the office, with all its noise and distraction, and then spend the rest of their time however they choose.

Sharing the work should not take longer than doing the work

Choose accountability and tools for 'working out loud' with care, and a view to the work itself. Some work roles lend themselves to quite automated systems, allowing you to oversee productivity on some kind of dashboard, as projects move through a typical cycle. Other things might need a bit more creative thought. It is too easy to wind up with a system which creates friction and adds to the work, such as remembering to update a shared document each day.

Apps designed to help teams track their progress, such as 'I Done This', are easy to update daily; but do make sure they are not feeding that defensive 'look at me and all the things I have done' mindset. No one should feel like they have to tick off a specific number of items, if they have spent the whole day (or month) working on one big, intangible and as-yet incomplete project.

Encouraging the habit of 'working out loud', whether people are planning, creating or directly executing work, can help team members to be accountable. If you use shared tools – for example, a Kanban-style board such as Trello or Planner – it's easy to maintain an overview of what you are working on, which anyone can examine if they want to see the status of something. Also, working in a shared environment such as Google Docs or Word Online, combined with real-time chat in Slack or Microsoft Teams, makes it easy to see who is doing what.

Once your team members relax into the freedom and autonomy of remote working, they will probably be among the many who find it hugely liberating. (If not, then look for alternatives – because a truly flexible manager should offer more than one option.) When objectives are well defined, trust is maintained, and everyone communicates effectively and appropriately – they will not get hung-up on needing to be seen to be 'busy' while working remotely. They can just enjoy being truly productive and effective.

Leadership reflections

If this chapter resonates with you and some of the behaviours and attitudes manifest in your team, you can take action to reorient things. The important thing is to recognise and decide to tackle it.

Here are some questions to discuss as a team.

1. How do we share our activities out loud, and is this working for everyone? How aware are we about what others are working on, and how much does it matter to us?

2. Are we mostly preoccupied with our own stuff, or paying careful attention to what other people are doing?

3. Do we have a sense of fair play about how work gets allocated, and how much effort everyone puts in? (Which is in no way to imply these things can or should be exactly equal across a team; rather, that there should be a sense that the hardest workers and highest performers are appropriately rewarded for this.)

Here are a few extra questions which you might find useful when discussing these issues one-on-one with team members, for example during performance reviews:

4. Do you feel that your manager sees and appreciates all that you contribute to the team and the work we are doing?

5. Do you ever feel that you are comparing your performance or visibility to that of other people, rather than the stated objectives of the work itself?

6. Are you happy with the way that your performance and contribution is managed and rewarded?

PART 2

REMOTE WELLBEING

5. PSYCHOLOGICAL SAFETY IN ONLINE MEETINGS

Feeling safe is an important prerequisite for doing our best work, otherwise our 'flight or fight' instincts will be yammering away at our brains, causing continual distraction. In the physical space we pay a lot of attention to health and safety and physical security requirements – but in every team, the importance of emotional safety is critical too.

In this chapter, Pilar explores some of the ways that we can nurture this in our online meetings, including specific things to be aware of in relation to the kind of technology we use – which can create barriers as well as bring people together, if we are unaware of all the potential pitfalls.

Psychological safety refers to:

> 'an individual's perception of the consequences of taking an interpersonal risk or a belief that a team is safe for risk taking in the face of being seen as ignorant, incompetent, negative, or disruptive. In a team with high psychological safety, teammates feel safe to take risks around their team members. They feel confident that no one on the team will embarrass or punish anyone else for admitting a mistake, asking a question, or offering a new idea.'[4]

In 2015, Google launched Project Aristotle with the aim of identifying the behaviours of managers that promote psychological safety in teams. The HR practitioners wanted to understand individuals' behaviours in high-performance teams, and so searched for data on the interactions contributing to success.

One of the activities where the research took place was team meetings. The researchers were expecting high-performance teams to share practices such as whether members caught up with non-work-related matters before the meetings, or whether they reviewed the work periodically, or whether

---

4   Google Re:Work (nd) 'Understand team effectiveness: Identify dynamics of effective teams'. Available at: https://rework.withgoogle.com/guides/understanding-team-effectiveness/steps/identify-dynamics-of-effective-teams/

they kept the content of the meetings completely business-focused. None of these or other practices were common to all teams.

The researchers only found only one common practice among all the high-performing teams: they had developed group norms that "created a sense of togetherness while also encouraging people to take a chance". They had developed psychological safety, a concept first identified and studied by Novartis Professor of Leadership and Management at Harvard University, Amy Edmondson.

The research also showed that these team managers and leaders shared a set of behaviours:

- They invited people to speak up.
- They talked about their own emotions.
- They didn't interrupt others.
- When someone was concerned or upset, they showed that it was OK to intervene.
- They tried to anticipate how people would react, and then worked to accommodate those reactions.

Creating the conditions for psychological safety in online meetings

The advice on managing teams that came out of Project Aristotle has been neatly summarised by Charles Duhigg in *Smarter, Faster, Better*.[5] Although the advice was targeted mainly at those running colocated team meetings, there is nothing to prevent you from adopting some (or all) of those behaviours in your online gatherings.

Let's have a look at some of Duhigg's suggestions, and how we might adopt them to the online environment.

Avoid interrupting team members

Not interrupting others can be harder in online meetings than in colocated ones. How many times have you interrupted someone due to a delay in the connection? One easy way of reducing interruptions is

---

5   Charles Duhigg (2016) *Smarter, Faster, Better: The Secrets of Being Productive*, William Heinemann.

to ask everyone to speak at the beginning of each meeting, so that you can assess the quality of their broadband and how well your meeting platform is operating.

If you engage in conversation, you can also practise adapting your rhythm to accommodate any delays in the connection. Ask each other questions, and see whether there are any gaps in the conversation caused by the technology.

(I have great fun assessing the quality of phone lines and other communication infrastructures during news items involving foreign correspondents, just by paying attention to the pauses as the sound comes through with a few seconds' delay.)

In addition to this, remember that silences feel longer in the online space. Someone pausing for breath, or trying to articulate a thought, might come across as having finished speaking. If in doubt, you can always say something along the lines of: "Can I double check that you've finished what you were saying?"

Admit what you don't know
Here is where we are at an advantage in the online space. We can admit that we don't know something; but if we know where to click on our browser or computer to top up our knowledge, we can find the answer almost straightaway. If someone asks something that you can quickly check while you are online, go ahead and check it.

Be sure to communicate what you are doing ("I don't know the answer to that, but if you give me ten seconds..."), and take a minute to look it up – while you mute yourself to prevent your typing from echoing loudly in your team members' ears.

Actually, even a minute might be too long. If it's going to take you more than 30 seconds to find an answer, you might as well make a note, look it up straight after the meeting, and add your findings to the online space where you follow up after meetings.

Don't end a meeting until everyone has spoken at least once
There are many reasons why people stay quiet in meetings – whether they are over audio, video or colocated. Sometimes people feel as if everything that had to be said, has been said – and they follow the ancient piece of advice:

"Don't speak unless you can improve the silence." (I first came across this nugget of wisdom in a fortune cookie.)

On other occasions, they might want the meeting to be over so that they can take a break from their computers. Moreover, it could be the case that they have not quite formulated their thoughts, and are not ready to share them.

Sometimes, before moving the conversation along, you might need to hold the silence to give room for people to speak up. Silence feels more uncomfortable in the online space, as people tend to stare at the screen when they are on video, and it is difficult to decipher what silence signifies during audio calls.

Be brave. Hold that silence after you have asked if anyone has anything further to add. Count to five if you must, even to ten. It might be the moment that the person who has not yet spoken decides to share their thoughts.

If you are meeting only over audio, keep an ear out in case someone has been very quiet for a long while. If you are concerned that certain members are being too quiet, you can have a list of people's names by you, and make a note of how often people speak.

In addition to helping you judge whether the conversation is being dominated by some individuals, there are practical reasons for checking if someone has been quiet for too long. You never know when someone's connection might drop off, or when a headset can suddenly stop working. Having a back-channel (such as an instant messaging chat) can be useful not only for sharing links and auxiliary thoughts, but also for pinging people discreetly, to check that they are still on the call.

One other way of ensuring that everyone speaks at the meeting is to do a 'round robin' in the team before ending. If you are on video, you can ask each person to nominate who should go next. If you are on audio, grab the list of names that you should have by your side, and ask the quieter folk to go first. Make sure that you have ticked everyone's name off that list before you close the meeting.

Your communication should not end with the meeting. If someone has something they still want to say after it has ended (for example, because time was running out or they did not want to hold everyone back), there should be a place only a click away where they can tell the rest of the team. The fact that the meeting has ended doesn't mean that you should stop the conversation.

More important than whether everyone has actually spoken or not at the meeting is that people know that they are allowed and welcome to speak out – and that they have had the opportunity to do so. Thanking people for their contributions, especially when it is obvious that they are struggling to articulate their thoughts or share an unpopular opinion, goes a long way.

Encourage people to share their frustration without being judged

This is really difficult to do – but again, one where we are at an advantage in the online space. Sometimes we can't help it. When people express their frustration at something that is not working in the team, we can feel personally attacked.

If online meetings are held on video, a disadvantage is that you can constantly see everyone and their reactions. In the colocated space you can only take in a few faces at a time, but in the online world (at least for now, while we're using 2D video), we are looking straight at everyone, all the time.

So in some cases, if you hear someone expressing discontent, just double check that you are not frowning, or responding in a way that might signal that it is not all right to continue speaking. Or if you catch yourself disapproving (sometimes we can't help it), focus on the questions you can ask them to understand the problem further.

Take a deep breath, focus on what they are saying (rather on the effect that the words are having on you), and ask as many questions as you can to comprehend their context.

(It's also worth remembering that in most cases, those in the meeting will not be able to see the lower half of our bodies. If discomfort or impatience creeps in when someone else is speaking, how about letting it flow to your legs instead of your face?)

A similar note of warning could be given for the audio-only space. Voice reflects the speaker's emotion, so be aware that the tone of your reply to someone expressing their frustration does not signal that such contributions aren't welcome.

Call out intergroup conflicts, and resolve them through discussion

One could argue that it is not the manager's responsibility to resolve all conflicts in the team. It should be the team's responsibility to resolve their own conflicts. In addition, you could suggest that if managers point out and resolve conflicts all the time, team members will always wait for the manager to act when there is conflict between people, rather than resolve it themselves.

This is an aspect beyond the scope of this book – only you know the make-up of your team. You will have to be the judge of when it is necessary for you to call out intergroup conflicts and resolve them through open discussion during your team's operations. However, at meetings, it is quite easy to see how the group is reacting to any conflict or disagreements.

I want to focus on the second noun – 'disagreements' – rather than 'conflict', as it is more specific. What looks like conflict to you might look like healthy discussion to me. However, if people are disagreeing and you are wondering whether to intervene, ask yourself:

- Is this discussion helpful to the work?
- Will it help us get better results, or improve our team process?
- Is this a discussion that we need to hold right now, or should those involved schedule a time to seek agreement – or at least an understanding?

Disagreements are helpful when they lead to actions or decisions. Otherwise, they are just social activities.

It is important to remember that disagreeing with team members about the work is an essential part of improving our process. Help people stay focused on the task, and notice how their disagreements help team members become even better at both collaboration and their work.

Leadership reflections

If you are leading online meetings you have a lot to think about, and this chapter will have given you plenty more. Ask yourself:

1. Am I comfortable with all the technology I am using to run my meetings? If I am distracted by the settings and whether everything is working OK, will I have the mental bandwidth to pay attention to all of the above? (Perhaps I

should practice first and get really familiar with the tools, or find something more intuitive.)

2. Am I allowing enough time for the meeting?

Online meetings can be very efficient from a time point of view, particularly compared with those involving travel. But to let everyone speak up, and silences take their rightful place with nobody feeling rushed, we do need to ensure people block out enough time and have clear expectations, to engage fully with the meeting.

3. Am I bringing my own issues into the room, to the detriment of the rest of the team?

As a team leader, you also deserve psychological safety, but in holding the emotional space for the rest of the team, be careful not to project your own 'stuff'.

6. IS WORK CAUSING YOU STRESS? GOING REMOTE IS NOT A MAGIC PILL

In this chapter, Maya talks about how our work location affects our wellbeing, and the impact of this on the teams and organisations in which we work. Managers and teams should constantly revisit their work habits, particularly when making the transition to remote.

We need to accept the fact that in its traditional form, work has some things wrong with it. It's making us ill for a start.

In Chapter 7 we will cover the challenges of managing seasonal sickness absence in colocated versus distributed workplaces, but not every sickness comes with an easily visible and curable set of symptoms. The most recent data from a Health and Safety Executive survey[6] shows that work-related stress, depression or anxiety accounted for 44% of work-related ill health and 57% of working days lost in 2017/18.

Why are we so stressed?

A number of factors potentially contribute to this statistic. Research usually cites anxiety and worry in the face of financial and job insecurity, as well as increased pressure to get more done in less time – possibly also to earn less in real terms by way of reward. Global political uncertainties may well contribute to escalated background stress levels, meaning that everyone is closer to reaching dangerous thresholds.

Many workers and managers are inclined to attribute increased workplace moans and groans to the daily commute, particularly at times of year when transport companies traditionally announce fare increases to coincide with horrible weather – which tends to create delays and disruption.

---

6   Health and Safety Executive (2018) 'Work related stress depression or anxiety statistics in Great Britain, 2018, October. Available at: www.hse.gov.uk/statistics/causdis/stress. pdf?utm_source=govdelivery&utm_medium=email&utm_campaign=digest-8-nov-18&utm_ term=report&utm_content=stress-stats

A further factor stressing commuters is that nowadays, a couple of hours a day spent rattling through suburbia is mostly regarded as additional work time, judging by the number of devices in use on public transport. A decade ago, you would look around and see people enjoying books and newspapers, but today everyone seems to be tapping at a keyboard or screen of one size or another.

So, happiness comes from working from home?

Of course, developing a policy of remote or flexible working can eliminate the daily commute to the office. But does it really make people happier and healthier?

The answer is: it definitely can.[7] Not being woken by an alarm clock before dawn to embark on a lengthy, expensive and uncomfortable journey is regarded by most as an immediate gain in the quality-of-life stakes.

While developing a dependable morning routine offers many physical and emotional health benefits, being able to create this around your preferred activities and start times offers a much greater sense of agency than being driven by the clock. This autonomy, this ability to choose, helps us to build resilience and derive better intrinsic motivation from our work.

As a manager, conferring trust on a team member to manage their time and work effectively from their preferred location shows them that you value their results and output, and want them to be able to focus on their work in the environment of their choice. However, it's not enough to simply send people home and expect everyone to instantly reap the benefits of this freedom effectively, or even beneficially.

Designing a strategy for wellness

Building healthy habits to support remote working takes specific, deliberate action, and a lot depends on the individual knowing their own needs when it comes to wellness and wellbeing.

For example, that walk to the station your team member used to moan about – and is so grateful to give up – may have been their main source of

---

7   Vitality (2017) 'Long commutes costing firms a week's worth of staff productivity, 22 May. Available at: www.vitality.co.uk/media/long-commutes-costing-a-weeks-worth-of-productivity/

exercise in a day spent mostly at a desk. Replacing it with a lie-in is brilliant in principle, and might lead to greater alertness and productivity later on; but the physical activity lost needs to be replaced too, otherwise your colleague may develop health problems which affect their work before too long.

Moreover, getting together in the break room to moan about rail strikes may have felt like negativity in the colocated office, but those shared conversations represented a source of connection and sympathy over which people could relate. Depending on where an individual is located on the extroversion–introversion scale, they might derive a lot of energy and motivation from that everyday chit-chat – much of it unrelated to the work itself – which the shared office space brought.

This is one reason why adopting a flexible 'office-optional' approach to a remote working transition can be the most considerate and effective way to support the wellbeing of an entire team. Encouraging those who need the buzz of a shared environment to base themselves at a local co-working hub can help to avoid isolation, and be part of the support package offered for colleagues moving to virtual working. The costs are far lower than the office rental saved, and may even leave budget over to maintain some shared meeting rooms or hot-desking space centrally.

Other people like working from coffee shops and cafés, just to experience that environment of being in a shared space. Companies such as MeetEdgar (whose dynamic CEO, Laura Roeder, was featured on our podcast),[8] offer specific expenses to support this in recognition of the measurable benefits it brings to their productivity and engagement.

For others who enjoy certain aspects of networking, but truly thrive on the peace and independence of working from their own home, supporting involvement in online communities might be the answer. This is why it's worth nurturing in-house groups in social enterprise networks and organising online learning events. (In addition to looking out for appropriate online communities open to the public, search for 'Slack group + [your industry]' for inspiration.) All the benefits of social contact, gossip, sharing problems and ideas, and new collaboration and connection opportunities – but you provide your own coffee, and keep your slippers on.

---

8   Virtual Not Distant (2018a) 'WLP152 – Clarity and Transparency at MeetEdgar', podcast, 11 January. Available at: www.virtualnotdistant.com/podcasts/meet-edgar

Managing the stress that still exists in a remote team

As a manager, do remember that just because you cannot see the long faces in the office any more, or get to listen to the rants about how many people were crammed on their delayed bus, shifting your team to remote working will not automatically relieve their work-related stress.

Stress comes from many sources:

- personal domestic circumstances
- health concerns
- relationships
- frustrations and difficulties with the work itself.

Providing a choice of environment and location may well offer great benefits to everyone's health and happiness, provided that it is managed well and takes everyone's needs into account.

Remember too, that picking up on signs of stress in the workplace can be much more difficult when you don't get to look people in the face on a daily basis. You will need to develop your own leadership skills and communication practices to ensure that problems are not overlooked until they escalate to dangerous levels. You can never assume that just because someone is not bringing up issues of concern directly that those issues are not present: you will need to develop ways of assessing emotional mood at a distance as part of your management role.

Leadership reflections

When did you last have an open discussion about stress and its effects within your team? Here are some things you might want to consider.

1. How psychologically safe do you and your team feel, when it comes to discussing vulnerabilities and our own needs?

What do people expect as a reaction, if they share a concern about their own physical or emotional health?

2. Do you as a leader ever find yourself failing to pay attention to the quieter ones – and in your own busy life and work, allowing yourself to assume that no contact means that nothing is wrong?

(This can be really dangerous in teams where you don't get direct feedback from being in eye contact regularly. Even if you have to set a private reminder to check in on everyone every few days, you have to make sure that you are doing it.)

3. Are you certain that when it comes to judgements about workload, stress and perceptions of ability and coping, remote and colocated workers are treated with fairness?

7. SICK AND TIRED, WORKING AND NOT-WORKING IN A REMOTE TEAM

In this chapter, Maya reminds us that people in remote teams also get sick, but that sick leave might be more difficult to take. This not only affects remote teams, in our omni-screen work–life blend today.

I can remember coming in on the tail-end of a telephone conversation many years ago, the last time I worked in a colocated office. A colleague was talking on an external line:

"No, don't worry, we'll find out about that and deal with it, you just concentrate on getting well. It's fine. Poor you, keep warm and rest – let me know when you can about tomorrow. Take care."

Once the receiver was replaced, shortly followed by: "Oh heck, Carol's off sick. That's a pain, today of all days!"

And it was.

Despite working in a shared office building, all of us had distinct roles and responsibilities, and while we nattered frequently about non-work things, updating everyone else on our autonomous project work happened mainly in scheduled meetings.

So exactly what needed doing on Carol's stuff this morning was far from obvious, even to her line manager. And poor Carol, huddled under her duvet with her medicine of choice, had no access to office files or documents – not even to email, which was pretty new to us then.

Being 'off sick'

Presumably, Carol had woken to her alarm as usual on a dark November morning, and made a judgement call. She was a diligent, hard-working project manager who had been nursing a cold all week – but that day she felt extra rough and had an escalating fever.

Out of courtesy to her colleagues, she knew she had to decide pretty early on whether to come into the office or not. Should she get up and make herself presentable, then face a commute involving a brisk walk and two underground trains, taking just over an hour, when she felt like this? Given the times and distances involved – and hers was below-average for Central London – she chose the paracetamol and her bed, and who can blame her?

It was extra hassle for her manager, and indeed for all of the rest of us, to cancel her meetings and contact some clients, but we knew she would do the same for us. And who even knew whether she would be back in tomorrow?

Meanwhile, perhaps it would be worth picking up some fizzy vitamin C drink or something at lunchtime, because Carol had been sniffing into tissues all week, around our workplace with its shared refreshment facilities, central heating and meeting rooms. The department would be in big trouble if anyone else went down with the flu.

Sickness absence and remote teams

It is hardly surprising then, that remote teams have a measurably lower rate of overall sickness absence than colocated ones – as high as 68% improvement.[9] Furthermore, when a commute to a distant office is involved, inevitably the absence has to be measured in whole days, even for things such as a scheduled appointment which happens at an inconvenient time. Home-based workers find it far easier to log back on again if they feel better a couple hours later, and not lose the entire day.

Indeed, every manager knows that an undefined proportion of 'off-sick' days are not quite what they appear on the face of it. Most businesses still do not have a policy or culture of emergency personal leave: as such, if an employee has a domestic or family emergency to deal with, the only way they might be able to handle it is to call in sick at work; whereas a home-based worker can keep an eye on their sick kids, or wait for the plumber, without any drop in their productivity.

9　Global Workplace Analytics (2015) 'Costs and benefits'. Available at: http://globalworkplaceanalytics.com/resources/costs-benefits

However, it would be a mistake to blithely assume that a remote team equals fewer days off sick, and that is all you need to think about.

While some of that 68% difference can be explained by spurious 'sickies' and reduced exposure to viruses in the office and on public transport, remote workers still become unwell from time-to-time. So, remote teams which have negligible recorded sickness absence might need to look a little more closely at what is really happening.

Balancing needs and commitments

One of the greatest reported drawbacks to working from home is a blurring of boundaries between work and home life. When managing acute or chronic illness, this can have both positive and negative consequences. Sure, you don't have to decide first thing in the morning whether to be off sick or not, but perhaps that would be much harder to do anyway?

If your work can be literally done from your bed, how ill do you have to be before you feel you can say that you are unfit to do it?

And when you have access to work files, email and collaboration tools via the smartphone on your bedside table, it is pretty much expected that however close you are to death's door, you will at least put the fires out before taking yourself offline for the rest of the day – divert calls, rearrange diaries and rapidly brief colleagues on emergency action on crucial projects, even asynchronously. Plus, you don't have to worry about spreading your germs over your internet connection.

Of course, this makes the absence far easier to manage organisationally, and might make it easier to take badly-needed rest with a clearer conscience. But for knowledge-workers these days, it becomes increasingly difficult to genuinely unplug from it all, when that might be what is badly needed.

Reading the signals

For managers of remote teams, it can be much harder to spot and deal with impending or complicated health problems. Going back to Carol: her manager, however frustrated, was not entirely surprised when she rang in sick because she had been looking like hell all week. Indeed, if she had dragged herself in that morning, it is quite likely that someone would have sent her straight home again as soon as they set eyes on her – and that is the one thing which does not tend to happen in a virtual team.

In virtual or remote teams, people have to tell their colleagues what is going on for them, and how they feel. This means that the manager – indeed, the whole organisation – has a responsibility to create a culture where that is genuinely safe and OK to do. A team where people can bring their whole self to work, the good and the really-not-so-good-today, in a non-judgemental setting. A team where people are trusted to judge when they need to take the day off because they are not well enough to work.

For hybrid organisations, the matter can be further confused by a perception that working from home is a kind of easier or soft option. In the UK, remote working is often considered as a 'reasonable adjustment' under the Equalities Act 2010 for staff suffering from stress and depression, or managing chronic illness. The 'Fit Note' (which replaced the 'sick note'), or the Return to Work Plan offered by Fit for Work,[10] provides options for people to continue working in a different capacity instead of going off sick entirely – working from home is one of these options.

While this has many benefits for people whose health or disability makes accessing a traditional workplace challenging, we contend that all the benefits of remote work should be available to everyone who wants it, and that it most certainly does not correlate with 'taking things easy'.

True equality surely means each person being able to define their own needs: for a working environment, team communications and meaningful professional activity. Being able to say "I have flu, I am unplugging for at least the next three days" or "I have a headache, hopefully I will catch up this evening, but for now I can't look at a screen" without any defensiveness or expectation of judgement. Or, in Carol's case, without the need to put on that slightly weak, wobbly, tired-sounded voice that doubtless she found herself unnecessarily adopting, when she rang in that morning.

If you are having one of those 'rubbishy' days, at least you do not have to haul out to commute in the dark. Wrap up warm, take plenty of fluids, and keep your germs to yourself. The chances are, you will be back on your feet more quickly than your commuting colleagues and ready to get back to work – but not before you *are* truly ready.

---

10   Fit for Work is a government-funded initiative in the UK, aimed at supporting employers and employees to help those who are in work with health conditions or off sick.

Leadership reflections

As a team leader, reflect on your own behaviour and attitudes, and how they affect psychological safety within your team when it comes to taking time off sick.

1. Do you model the behaviour you expect by being open about your own needs, asking for help when you are feeling poorly, and taking time off when needed?

Encouraging open conversations about physical and mental health, and acknowledging how that affects the work, is important. As is saying to colleagues: "I am logging off the shared drive now, and will put out of office on my personal inbox for the rest of the day", so everyone else knows that it is definitely OK when they need to do so.

2. Do you encourage people to bring their whole selves to work, and share what is going on for them, good and bad?

Fostering that closeness and concern, and making individuals visible as well as their work, helps everyone anticipate good and bad days in themselves and in others – and for managers, it means fewer surprises.

3. Do you help people protect their boundaries and meet their own needs, by not rewarding martyrdom and self-sacrifice, encouraging them to take the time they need to be happy and well when they need to?

You can signal this by calling out good examples in other team members publicly – "Remember, Anna's going to be blasting through her reports today, as she has to leave early for her theatre group" – and dealing privately with any insecurities or productivity issues with specific individuals.

PART 3

HOW ARE WE DOING?

8. SHARING SUCCESS IN REMOTE TEAMS

'Blowing your own trumpet' and celebrating personal success might be more difficult on a remote team, and requires calling things out yourself rather than getting noticed by others. In this chapter, Pilar examines some of the ways you can mitigate this with thoughtful action.

In the article '3 Ways You Are Failing Your Remote Workers',[11] Gallup researchers note that "fully remote workers are 29% less likely to strongly agree that they have reviewed their greatest successes with their manager in the past six months".

The reasons given by the study are that:

- Workers don't want to look like they are blowing their own trumpet by sharing their success, which often results in managers and other team members not being aware of the great things that people are doing.
- Managers do not want to take up too much of their people's time, and so tend to keep their catch-ups short.

As with all communication in the remote space, we need to be deliberate when we talk about success. Employees cannot rely on managers and others just picking up on the fact that they are competent at their jobs; and managers cannot always rely on others telling them the great things they have been up to – team members need to inform, and managers need to ask questions.

Fuelling intrinsic motivation and learning from success

Deci and Ryan's Self-Determination Theory[12] suggests that people's desire to do their best is driven by a sense of autonomy, competence and relatedness.

---

11   Annamarie Mann (2017) '3 Ways You Are Failing Your Remote Workers', Gallup, 1 August. Available at: www.gallup.com/opinion/gallup/214946/ways-failing-remote-workers.aspx

12   See 'Self-Determination Theory', available at: http://selfdeterminationtheory.org

Reviewing our greatest success with someone else can increase our sense of connection with others, as well as helping with our feeling of competence.

It is not only satisfying to be able to share that we are doing our job well, but during our conversations with others we might identify ways of learning from, or building on, those successes that we had not thought of in the first place.

Don't ask, don't tell

If we don't inform others of our results, they might never find out. If we don't ask people what they have recently achieved, or the aspect of their work of which they are most proud, they might never tell us.

It is an effort to remember to have these conversations, so why not make them part of your team's commitments to each other? Find regular ways of catching up with each other's achievements so that it becomes part of your team's practice.

The Gallup article recommends carrying out this recognition in team meetings, weekly emails or scheduled check-ins. Here are some other suggestions:

- Committing to posting recognition of someone else's achievement once a week in your collaboration platform (for those of you who enjoy incorporating bots into your tools, you could even have a bot that reminds you once a week to post).
- Highlighting or using a different font colour for successes when 'working out loud' or reporting on work done.
- Having a regular slot in review meetings where individuals share something they have done, of which they are proud.

"But I don't like sharing so much"

Think about it: it's good for you that other people know what you are achieving, and to share why you are proud of a piece of work – it might take you closer to identifying what you want to work on next. Plus others can learn from hearing someone talk of success.

However, not everyone is comfortable sharing their achievements. If that is the case and you want to shift the focus away from yourself, place it instead on what you have achieved. Talk about your process, not just your results. For example:

- What helped you?
- What stood in your way?
- If you have tackled similar tasks or projects before, what did you do differently this time?

Similarly, as a manager, if you want to show appreciation for somebody's good work, don't just stop at 'Well done!' Find out more about the conditions which helped your team member be successful, what helps them to do a great job. Turn it into a learning opportunity to help the whole of your team's performance.

Let technology help you

Some of us are happy to have these personal conversations on video (I consider talking about how I work quite personal, even if it's work-related), while others prefer to use audio-only. Meanwhile, some are only really comfortable typing these conversations.

So, review your communication methods:

- What do people prefer?
- What do individuals prefer for their one-on-ones?
- What can you agree on using as a team?

Your preferences as manager might well be taking over how the team operates, so be aware of what they are, and make sure that you are not imposing on others what works best for you.

Don't forget: you are a team

It's a shame to restrict the 'success conversation' to the manager–employee relationship. One of the opportunities that virtual teamwork offers is that of creating flatter structures in organisations. People can work autonomously (provided that they have the information and resources they need), and should require less hand-holding and supervision than in traditional workplaces.

Opening up the 'success conversation' to the whole team can lead to shared learning, high morale and a team culture of responsibility and accountability. (Please note that I say '*can* lead': this might not work with team members used to rigid hierarchies, or who are not comfortable sharing their work.)

When operating as a remote team, we have permission to formalise the spontaneous, so why not deliberately create the conditions for success conversations to take place?

Agreeing on a simple way for team members to share their achievements with each other is one way of letting people know that it's OK to blow your own trumpet, and keep everyone updated on the progress of the work. (I have added this last one for those managers who like to keep their conversations short. In this way, you don't need to ask your team member if they have something successful to share with you – you can go straight into congratulating them for it.)

An example of how some 100% distributed companies are already doing this comes from Convert.com. Morgan Legge, Holacracy® Bootstrapper and Facilitator and HR Champion at the company, once shared with me:

> We recently started a #humblebrag channel and also a casual weekly Wins & Miseries video chat with the whole team. Even though we had Buddy Calls, we needed a more structured approach to solicit and implement feedback on the work we produce.[13]

Working in a remote team is not always easy or fun. As with all teams, at some point our communication will break down: we might disagree with others and have uncomfortable conversations; we might even start wondering why we put up with building working relationships through technology at all.

Sharing success is rewarding: it boosts our morale, reminds us of our potential and can even increase trust. Reviewing our success can uncover hidden strengths, help us in the future, even be of use to someone else. Sharing and reviewing our success is one of the easiest parts of working with others, so it should not be left to chance.

---

13   Quoted from conversation in the private forum of the Virtual Team Talk community, 27 July 2017. Reproduced here with kind permission of Ms Legge.

Leadership reflections

Here are some things to think about.

1. When was the last time you shared and reviewed your greatest success with someone else?

If you don't lead by example, getting out of your own comfort zone as necessary, then you are not helping others to follow. So, get out that trumpet and give it a long blast when the time is right!

2. Would a structured way of doing this, such as a dedicated, success-sharing channel in your communication system or standard meeting agenda, enable people to share their achievements more broadly?

3. Are you learning from successes?

Abstracting from and modelling the conditions connected with success is a powerful way to both create continuous improvement, and reinforce behaviours and mindsets which serve everyone's motivations and goals.

However, don't let this detract from the moment of celebration itself! Savour the popping of champagne corks (or metaphorical online equivalent), before you dig into the analysis of it.

9. TO SHOW FRUSTRATION, FIRST YOU NEED TO SHOW YOU CARE

One of the most challenging aspects of leading a remote team is navigating through conflict, disagreement and difficult situations. In this chapter, Pilar shows how she has learned from first-hand experience the value of working on team relationships at all times, not just when things go wrong.

Most advice about how to have difficult conversations in virtual teams starts too late in the process: at the point when we are obliged to have the conversation because disagreement, or even conflict, has surfaced. Avoiding conflict altogether is not the answer: often, disagreement and some types of conflict are beneficial to a team. They bring different viewpoints into the decision-making process, remind us that we are accountable to each other, and are a sign that people care about the work.

But conflict is intrinsically uncomfortable. We have all experienced those occasions where we can't wait for a meeting to be over because someone else is driving us crazy, when we are going round in circles without finding common ground, and when silence makes us uncomfortable.

We know that these things will happen in any group relationship, so it makes sense to be prepared. And being prepared means working hard at building strong relationships with our teammates long before we get to that point – all the time, not just when things become difficult.

Start with regular communication

I really wish I could give you some other, groundbreaking advice. However, too often – and especially in hybrid teams, where some team members work together in the office, while others are remote – communication with remote employees only takes place when we need something specific from them or something goes wrong. We see interacting with our colleagues as having a cost in some way, as requiring more effort than with someone sat in the same room, so we tend to get in touch with them more sparingly and less casually.

Even at the team level, unless we have a culture of meeting regularly and 'working out loud' online, our conversations will be very task-focused. This is great to get the work done efficiently, but it doesn't help us to build relationships or to learn about what motivates, inspires or annoys our colleagues either – all things which ultimately facilitate the work.

Online meetings which focus only on getting through the agenda miss out on providing the space for people to express their values, fears and aspirations. Focusing too rigidly on getting straight to the point can mean that we miss out on an opportunity to find out a little bit more about each other – not necessarily through insights such as what someone had for lunch or dinner (although some people find that to be an important point of connection) – but through making space for laughter to emerge, expressing our doubts and struggles, and sharing those moments we are proud of in a space where we feel psychologically safe to do so (as mentioned previously in Chapter 5).

Building an environment where spontaneous interactions can take place goes a long way towards building strong relationships. In the online space we should not be wary of having a 10- minute chat with someone about very little in particular, just as one might hang around in a corridor talking to someone for a few minutes to catch up. In the same way, we should feel comfortable letting people know when an interruption is unwelcome.

The road to open conversations

The core idea behind Kim Scott's book *Radical Candor*[14] is that we are better able to challenge our team members when they already know that we care deeply about them. In order to build that kind of relationship, we need to work at it: by regularly checking in with each other, having conversations about our values, sharing our work (and other things about ourselves), and showing interest in the work and lives of others.

---

14   Kim Scott (2017) *Radical Candor: How to Get What You Want by Saying What You Mean*, Macmillan.

The personal touch

As most of my writing is inspired by personal experiences, allow me to share what prompted this chapter.

I had been working with an organisation for almost a year. My engagement started with a coaching requirement for the project manager and before I knew it, I was pulled into the virtual team in charge of piloting a new way of working in the company.

I worked very closely with the project manager, and we understood each other incredibly well. She had been working and growing her personal capacity in the online space, and knew the importance of checking in with people regularly, moving from text-based to voice communication when conversations got tricky, and creating the space for team members to get to know each other as people, not just colleagues.

We shared similar values and the vision for the project and company, and spent many hours talking about the world of work – in particular, about the concept of virtual teamwork.

However, we reached a point in the project where everything was changing. We tried out many different things in the pilot and on top of that, were working in an organisation where things also kept changing with very little warning. We were right in the middle of an almost chaotic change process.

In one conversation, the project manager and I simply didn't understand each other. I was having trouble pinpointing how we should adapt our strategy, and she couldn't see a reason to change our plans.

At one point she said, "I'm getting really frustrated with you."

As difficult as it was to hear, I welcomed it as a very important piece of information. Prior to that, we had gone through long silences in our conversation, long monologues, clicking away at files trying to make a point – so for someone to articulate what was going on emotionally for us was very useful.

She named how we were both feeling, and that meant we could adjust our conversation accordingly. But she was only able to be candid because she knew her words would land well. In the past, we had had many conversations, also moments when we had disagreed, but we reflected on what was going on. We came back to each other, understood each other and moved forward.

Without all those earlier moments when we had laughed about the things that frustrated us in general, complained about other people who were driving us mad, celebrated our small achievements and shared reflections which, while not about our personal lives, were actually quite personal – we would not have been able to have had that candid conversation.

We learned together from experience – that a good working relationship will always bring with it difficult moments.[15]

It is worth being prepared for those times when our happy, remote team is hit by difficult situations. It is way too easy to deal with an emotional situation by switching off our computers, so in the remote space we have to work twice as hard.

Leadership reflections

Every aspect of the team's culture and performance stems from the example that you as the leader sets; this applies to the way that we disagree with one another too (and how we create the acceptance that disagreement is OK). Consider these questions in relation to your own practice.

1. What kind of conversations do I have with my team members? Are there plenty of opportunities to show them I care – to take an interest in their work, even when I am not following up their progress or need anything from them?

2. If someone were to ask my colleagues: 'Does [insert your own name] care about me as much as the work?', what response would I expect?

Do I genuinely take an interest in them in a way that goes beyond delivering their agreed outputs and commitments?

3. As a team, how often do I and my team members check in with each other, even if we don't have a work-related question, or need to provide feedback?

---

15   When I asked the project manager whether she was OK with me publishing this anecdote, as well as agreeing, she added that she was able to share her frustration due to a profound feeling of trust, while also allowing herself to push that trust to the edge.

If you sense a need to create changes here, you might need to engineer shifts in the ecosystem of apps and tools that you use, working practices or other practical things, but don't let these be a distraction from the need to change the level of care expressed, which is what really matters.

10. CREATING A CULTURE OF FEEDBACK

Hands up: who loves giving and receiving feedback? It's often difficult to hear and accept input on our performance and activities and what we could be doing better. For online teams, it can be more challenging to create the structures and systems to support this. However, the benefits are many, and it is up to the leadership to set the expectation – on this, as in so many other things – as Pilar discusses in this chapter.

In *Originals*, Adam Grant shares an unusual story about a CEO:

'At the software company Index Group, CEO Tom Gerry asked a consultant to tell him everything he did wrong in front of his entire staff of roughly a hundred employees. By role modelling receptivity to feedback, employees across the company became more willing to challenge him – and one another.'[16]

Talk about leading by example and really creating a culture of feedback! As I was reading I was thinking, "How could this be translated into ongoing behaviour or practice, in a remote team?"

As if reading my mind, Grant – a professor of management at The Wharton School, University of Pennsylvania – went on to describe how he gathers anonymous feedback asynchronously from his students, focusing on "constructive criticism and suggestions for improvement". He then emails the full set of suggestions to the entire class and summarises the findings in the next session, inviting more feedback on his interpretation of the suggestions, as well as telling the students how he proposes to address the issues raised.

"That's an interesting idea," I thought. Personally, I am not a fan of anonymous feedback, and would not recommend that you regularly seek it in this way from your team – although I am aware that in some hierarchical

16   Adam Grant (2016) *Originals: How Non-conformists Change the World*, Virgin Digital, loc. 3152.

systems such as a university, it might be the only way of finding out what people really think.

However, I can see no better way for a manager to nurture a culture of feedback than by inviting it from team members (for example, via email or private message), and then sharing a condensed version of the comments in a meeting, a message or as an internal blog post, as well as how he or she will incorporate it into his or her work. Feedback can then turn into a conversation, rather than a one-directional approach.

Furthermore, considering how damaging a bad manager can be to a team and organisation, it is worth formalising how to receive feedback from team members.

I am not recommending that you immediately follow the examples above, but I do suggest you consider whether your team members could do with a more deliberate approach towards regularly reviewing their performance – and yes, that does include you as a manager. You are also a member of your team!

Make giving and receiving feedback easy

One of the dangers of working apart from other team members is that we find it difficult to gauge how we are doing. We start to wonder whether our work is any good, and whether we are contributing enough to the team. One of your responsibilities as a manager is to create a culture of feedback, and this applies whether you are colocated or remote.

Giving feedback is not something that many people enjoy, especially when asking someone to change their behaviour. When you are working with people remotely, it is always tempting to find something else that needs to be said, done or discussed. Unless there is a formal process in place (even if it is a get-together every three months, to check how we are doing), no one might receive any feedback on their work and behaviour until it is too late. Even then, if we only give feedback when something is wrong, we associate it with problems – so you can see where this all might lead.

There are systems and tools we can use to regularly give feedback on remote teams. As a manager, you can set a regular schedule to meet one-to-one (on audio or video). Set up these chats so they are conversations rather than one-way reports from either of you. Find out how team members are doing, what they are struggling with, what they are proud of, and what they need from you.

Mention any progress you have seen recently, or ask whether there are any blocks delaying progress. Point out any helpful team behaviours that have suddenly stopped, and find out what the reasons might be for this. Provide the space for them to celebrate what is going well too (see Chapter 8).

Stay on schedule

The most important thing about these one-to-ones is that they are regular, even if sometimes they only last five minutes. It is important for both of you to know that you have a slot where you can have uncomfortable conversations when you need to, rather than expecting a problem to be flagged every time that a one-to-one meeting is called.

If your team is a true team (that is, one in which people's tasks are interdependent, and people need to work together to achieve their goals), you will need some sort of system or set-up whereby team members can discuss how they are affecting each other's work, and how team members are functioning together.

As always, how you build your feedback system will depend on the nature of your team, and how individuals prefer to communicate and receive it. Here are some suggestions.

Set up a system

This needs to match different people on a one-to-one basis regularly, to meet up synchronously online.[17]

As a team, you can agree on a structure for these conversations so that you always know how to kick them off. You can adapt Automattic's '3-2-1-Oh' process, which I particularly like. It was created for the regular one-to-ones that managers have with their team members, but you could use it also for team members to check in regularly with each other. During the conversation, the team member reports on:

---

17   For an automated way of doing this, see Donut (www.donut.ai); for a more person-led system, see how Trello is used to match people up – it has now automated its system. Lydia M. (2015) 'How 15 minutes each week keeps our distributed team connected', Trello, 19 August. Available at: https://blog.trello.com/how-15-minutes-each-week-keeps-our-distributed-team-connected

- three things they have done well
- two areas or skills which need improvement
- one way in which the team lead and organisation can support them.

Finally, the 'Oh' brings one or two sentences on what they are most excited or grateful for in the organisation, and how they would like to develop their career.

Agree on a day of the week

This is a day where you send each other feedback (via direct message or email). If you are a small group (around five of you), you might want to do this for every person on your team; if you are a large group, divide yourselves into 'feedback circles' or pairs.

Have monthly or bimonthly online meetings as a team

Do this to review your process, not necessarily your results. Answer questions such as:

- Is communication effective?
- Do you feel supported?
- Are there any blocks you constantly come across?

Whether the answer to these is 'yes' or 'no', make sure that you ask why. (It is just as important to understand why something is working, so it can be sustained, as it is to identify exactly what needs to change.)

Give permission

Establish a way of giving permission for immediate feedback when witnessing team member behaviour that we find unhelpful. This might seem a bit odd, so let me give some context.

When we are working with someone in the same space, we often gather a lot of information about a person's current mood and their general state of mind. If we know them relatively well, it's easy to gauge whether they are in the mood to receive feedback, or even to listen to a bit of criticism.

When we work away from others, we lose a lot of this information. We can't see whether someone has had a really bad day, so our little hint at the fact that they never seem to be finishing a piece of work by the time they promised might just feel like they are being kicked when they are down.

Sometimes we feel like we can take any kind of feedback, and we welcome it. Other times, we feel like the universe is against us, and we just need to get through the next few weeks as best as we can.

For example, if you use a platform such as Slack, you can allocate an icon that represents the permission request. All the other team member then needs to do is to reply with a green icon or a red icon – or whatever your team agrees on. Only on a 'green light' reply do you then send your feedback.[18]

So, having a system whereby you first ask permission to give immediate, corrective feedback might be useful.

Don't forget your own development

Finally, as a manager, ask for feedback yourself. If you have difficulty framing the question, give it a different focus:

- Is there anything I could be doing to help your work?
- Are there times when you feel I am in your way?
- Are there any specific aspects of your work that you think could be improved?

You can even dare to ask, "Is there something I'm already doing that you want to make sure I sustain?" Yes, there might be things we are already doing well, so let's make sure we know what they are!

If you want to get regular feedback on how you can help your team members, you can adopt Automattic's '3-2-1-Oh' system, as described earlier

18 Credit for coming up with this also goes to Sam Mednick and Yoris Linhares, who were part of the Happy Melly team when I was working there and we were creating a system for giving feedback.

in this chapter. Having just talked about their own work, team members might be more prepared to give you feedback, or ask for help.

Leadership reflections

You can use the suggestions in this chapter to check the adequacy of your own arrangements, and see how you feel about taking a more structured approach to giving and receiving feedback within your own team.

Some questions you might want to discuss as a group include the following.

1. How comfortable do we all feel about receiving feedback – is it something we are intrinsically fearing and avoiding? Where did this feeling come from?

If you identify real sensitivity within some or all of the team, have a look at the ideas above for approaching spontaneous feedback and signalling readiness (or otherwise) to receive it.

2. Have our feelings changed about this, if we have transitioned to a more 'office-optional' working style?

Is there more of a sense that we should be left to get on with things and focus on results only, which goes along with the trust implicit in remote work? Or are we hiding behind our lack of direct visibility to avoid being frank with each other?

3. How truly two-way is the process, and are we all comfortable giving and receiving feedback in both directions – speaking 'truth to power' and asking for help where we need it?

How can we – or do we – show appreciation for the gift of feedback, even if the feedback itself is not what we were hoping for or expecting? How well do we acknowledge the time and attention and intent inherent in speaking up, especially when we know it has been even more uncomfortable to do so, given the message itself?

PART 4

LOOKING OUT

11. KEEPING YOUR TEAM VISIBLE WITHIN YOUR ORGANISATION

In this chapter, Pilar suggests a number of ways in which teams can maintain a high profile within their organisation.

When teams start to work in an 'office-optional' fashion, they consciously change their communication methods and frequency to make sure that they stay visible to each other, and so that information about the work itself does not fall through the virtual cracks.

Most advice given (and sought) by remote teams is about intra-team communication and the visibility of team members to other team members.

Teams don't live in isolation, so how do we remain visible within our organisation?

The first thing we need to think about is who we want to be visible to. Ask yourself:

- Who are those people that can help our team when we need a little inside information, or a favour from another part of the organisation?
- Who are the people who always seem to be on top of developments and changes in the company?
- Who are the people we would love to collaborate with at some point?
- Who are the people with whom we might start developing some sort of relationship?
- Who is on our radar that might come in useful at some point?

How will you find out who is driving collaborative projects across the organisation? You know how people get roped into them: by having a quick conversation in the lift, through overhearing something in the café.

How will you be able to tune into what is going on, and be visible enough so that they bear you in mind?

Visibility and beyond

When I talk about being visible in an organisation, I don't just mean making sure that others know what we are doing; but about managing to initiate and nurture relationships with other members of the organisation – even if we are unlikely to bump into them by the coffee machine.

When making the transition from operating fully in the office space, think about who, as a team and as individuals, you should remain connected to – as with most practices in the online space, you will need to be deliberate about this.

Make them visible

Start by mapping out your network. Who do you already know? Who has connections in your team to those in other areas? Create a large spider diagram, with names and team membership, and keep it somewhere it can be easily viewed and updated. Use a slide creating programme or a drawing tool; you can also use mind-mapping software or online sticky notes.

The important thing is that any of you can quickly find out that, for example: "Jane knows Sally in Marketing quite well – she's the one we should contact when we need to chase up the marketing data we need for our report."

When you share an office and the same schedules, you can easily turn around and ask out loud, "Do any of you know anyone in marketing who can send those numbers we're waiting for?" In the online space, it will be quicker and simpler to pull up the graphic which shows that Jane knows Sally. Then you can ask Jane directly to chase Sally up – or better still, message Jane openly in your collaboration platform, to avoid other team members chasing up after Sally too.

Be social

If your organisation has an enterprise social network, make sure you pop in there regularly. Have a look at what is being discussed and where there is most activity: see which groups might be meeting offline.

If posting 'Facebook-style' is not your thing, find a different way of interacting. If you want to reply to a specific person but are unsure about doing it publicly, do it privately. Send a direct message or email, or give them a call. I know that this is just one more thing to add to a busy schedule, but it's important to listen in, know what is going on and who is talking to whom.

Depending on your workplace, it might be worth spending some time on social media, paying attention to what people in your organisation are sharing. You might find interesting bits of information – people often post in the online world what they have experienced offline. These open networking sites can be a great source of information about people and what they are up to.

Last, but definitely not least...

Don't forget to advocate for what your team do: talk to others about who you work with and what you work on – about the detail of your work. Find opportunities to share your achievements through internal communications; attend events (both online and offline), even if they are not directly connected to your work.

As mentioned previously, I am not recommending that you should be blowing your own trumpet every day, but share what you are working on, what you are learning, the projects that you have completed successfully. Make sure that the contacts in other parts of the organisation who regularly work with your team know when someone new joins you, or is moving on. Onboard your newcomers not just into your team's communication systems, but also into your team's network.

If you have recently gone remote and left part of your network in the office, this is the perfect time to touch base to remind them that you are only a message, phone or video call away – there are many ways to bridge that physical distance.

Leadership reflections

The advocacy role is key to team leadership. Managers usually network with different people in the organisation – every conversation, interaction or email is an opportunity to make the team's work visible.

1. Think about how often you talk to others in the organisation about your team and your work, and the words and phrases you use. Is your 'team branding' positive and consistent?

2. Think about how you reach out to others in the organisation for help. Do you always contact the same people?

When you are looking for information, do you take that opportunity to expand your network, connecting to those with whom you want to build a stronger relationship?

3. How often do you and your team talk about how you want to be seen in the organisation, and whether there is any sense of a gap between what you want and the actual perception?

No one is suggesting hiring a marketing company to reposition you – but it's important to be conscious of your networking potential and visibility when you are leading a remote team within a larger organisation.

12. VIRTUALLY SECURE IS NOT ENOUGH: INFORMATION SECURITY CHALLENGES FOR REMOTE TEAMS

While we often talk about making our work visible, building trust and being great leaders to our remote teams, we rarely discuss the security issues surrounding our flexible set-up. In this chapter, Maya shares some friendly guidance on how to start the conversation with your team members and organisation.[19]

As virtual, flexible and remote working becomes increasingly commonplace for teams in a wide range of sectors, the benefits that this offers for improved productivity, motivation and work satisfaction are welcome. Technological changes, from mobile communications to cloud storage, have been a huge part of making this possible. However, those very technologies can create significant vulnerabilities when it comes to security and data protection.

In May 2018 the European Union (EU) implemented the General Data Protection Regulation (GDPR), bringing with it huge legislative changes. Managers had to liaise with information security departments to implement changes, while small business owners had significant new responsibilities of their own.

While *Virtual Not Distant* was not set up to provide legal advice of any kind, when GDPR was implemented, we suggested that every organisation review its policies and practice around data protection and privacy – especially if those policies had not been reviewed since people started working out of the office, or on their own devices. Things tightened up significantly under the regulation, and a few of the changes that organisations needed to be aware of included:

- the definition of 'personal data'
- increased sanctions and reporting requirements in relation to breaches

---

19   The content in this chapter is sourced from an article was originally published some months before the implementation of GDPR in Europe – a time during which, hopefully, a lot of organisations were reviewing their data protection and information security practices.

- an overall shift in responsibility to the data processor, and
- emphasis on the privacy rights of individuals.

Challenges for the remote environment

When everyone is colocated in a single space, it is much easier to control the way that data is transmitted, stored and processed, as well as being able to limit it to specific devices. But when we enable teams to work from wherever they choose, that comes at the cost of considerable control. When you bear in mind that the organisation itself retains legal responsibility for safe data processing, you will want to ensure that your systems are watertight.

Some of this will be common sense, and can be addressed through up-to-date information security policies, combined with training and regular review – it is not enough to simply issue documents of instruction to your team, because in the event of a serious breach, you will need to be able to demonstrate that these policies were fully understood and tested.

Working outside of the office does create new practical risks, and the more flexible and blended our lifestyles become, the more good practice can be seen as 'getting in the way' of flexibility. For example: two-factor authentication takes that little bit longer, quickly editing a document on a mobile device is so easy to do, and insecure public wifi is just so ubiquitous and available nowadays. So, it is vital that your procedures and training specifically address risky behaviours relevant to now, and make it clear what behaviours represent a breach of the organisation's policies.

Bring your own device: security versus flexibility for the flexible worker

Bearing human factors in mind, you can anticipate vulnerabilities and address them structurally. If people want to work on their tablets because they travel a lot, then providing everyone with access to a mobile virtual private network (VPN) is an inexpensive way to make this a great deal safer. If you suspect that a ban on USB devices will be hard to enforce, then issuing secure, encrypted flash drives (protected with a thumbprint or PIN) will ensure that your database isn't left on a bus – at least not in a format that anyone can access.

When people are using their own devices for work, as is increasingly the case, then a careful trade-off must be made between their own choices and privacy, and the security needs of the organisation. All of this requires an open dialogue and understanding on both sides, so your 'bring your own device' policy can accommodate reasonable limitations on exactly which own devices can be used, and in what way.

For example, if someone wants the convenience of being able to process data classified as 'sensitive' on behalf of their employer using their own mobile phone, then arguably the organisation's information security team should have the ability to completely reset that device remotely if it is lost or stolen. However, the same device obviously contains lots of personal content belonging to the employee, their photos, etc. – and they have their own rights to expect privacy from services such as location tracking.

Similarly, if someone wants to use their own laptop, it needs to be regarded as a 'mobile device' in terms of physical vulnerability – especially if working from different locations rather than just at home, and being carried around a lot. So, disk encryption and remote override will become mandatory, as will access control: you cannot process personal data on the same machine that your kids do their homework on – or at least not via the same profile login.

And let's not even get started on back-ups and cloud storage, because this is one of the biggest data security challenges facing information technology teams today: where exactly *is* the data? Different standards and regulations apply in different parts of the world, and if remote workers are backing up their own drives and devices in ways that you cannot control or understand, then it is far more likely that copies of personal data will end up where they shouldn't be.

The General Data Protection Regulation

From 25 May 2018, all entities processing data about any EU citizen had to ensure that their policies were in line with the new requirements, and that they were fully compliant – protecting the organisation, the remote worker, and ultimately the data subject whose information is being processed.

Conducting appropriate risk assessments, and encouraging a company culture of openness where breaches (or suspected breaches) can be safely disclosed and addressed, means that we can learn from them. Also, it fosters a culture where people respect privacy and data minimisation as intrinsic principles, and are not afraid to question anything perceived as risky. If the worst happens, the regulator will take into account how an organisation has responded to limit the damage and impact on data subjects – any kind of blame culture which encourages an individual to try to cover up or fix a breach on their own could have disastrous outcomes.

Put simply, there is no time for any individual to do this on their own: there has to be an absolute commitment to holding up hands at the merest suspicion of a problem, so that the right procedures can be followed (and seen to be followed). It means accurately maintaining a log of breaches and their outcomes. The organisations which are likely to be the first GDPR test cases will surely be those where people are afraid to admit a mistake, fear sanction and do not trust one another.

It is important that GDPR compliance is not used as an excuse to push back on remote working, or all the benefits that this brings to the organisation and the individual. So we must ensure that potential vulnerabilities are addressed in good time, by coaching and continuously improving practice. Choosing the right tools and addressing security concerns from the outset will enable our organisations to move forward safely and responsibly, as data protection falls under ever-greater public scrutiny.

Leadership reflections

These legislative changes, combined with a number of high-profile public breaches, mean that information security and data protection remain at the forefront of popular discourse. Organisationally, we can use this to progress conversations within our teams.

Here are some things you might want to consider and discuss.

1. Is compliance seen as a burden, extra hassle or something which gets in the way of the work? Or is the privacy of our stakeholders (clients, customers, colleagues) truly central to the work itself?

Privacy by design is the aspiration, but we all have to start from where we are now. If this means acknowledging that things are far from perfect, then at least it is a benchmark for improvement. Understanding exactly how the tools we use for our remote collaboration address this issue is a good beginning.

2. Can we have an honest conversation about whistleblowing and blame culture, if we need to?

The new legislation has strict deadlines and time frames for notification of breaches or losses, both to regulators and to those affected.

3. How does this feed into our learning process (see above)? Not only will regulators look for good logging of past incidents, but it is also reasonable to expect that they will not look favourably on repeated breaches of the same nature.

What can be done to prevent recurrence of the situation, and how is this being communicated to everyone who needs to learn from it?

13. REMOTE WORK: ANYTIME, ANYPLACE, ANYWHERE

This book concludes with a humorous reflection from Maya on a summer of 'digital nomading', which didn't turn out exactly as anticipated. Although as ever, there is always something to be learned!

I realised that this summer I have actually been working remotely for 18 years (as this phase of my life started with the birth of my eldest daughter, I now have a visible reminder who is considerably taller than I am). As such, you would reasonably expect that I would have got the work-remotely thing completely sorted out by now – at the very least I would feel some kind of 'coming of age', or a sense of being grown-up about it.

That was the feeling I needed this summer, when for complicated personal reasons I embarked on a month-long non-holiday – a period which included four countries, clearing and redecorating a house, a major speaking event and several important meetings.

"No problem", I thought confidently as I packed up my laptop, *"I can work from anywhere... I am liberated and laid back and ready for the road."* No more envying those unencumbered, twenty-something 'digital nomads' who wander the world in a haze of hotspots – this summer too I shall be truly flexible, and Get Things Done wherever I go. I was going to be unstoppable.

Oh, yes – and what was that, another meet-up? "Sure, let's get it in the diary, after all it's only a short way from where I'll be anyway, and I am *so* flexible..." I felt The Power of Remote.

The grown-up reality?

Massive overscheduling, tremendous stress, some very close-run risks of badly letting down clients, and proof that you are never too old to learn. Throw in a horrible London heatwave and a flight delayed for 20 hours... You get the picture.

The single biggest lesson that summer 2018 taught me, was that *yes*, when you really have to, you can work from anywhere – but all work is not created equal.

Now, this is something I would have said I was aware of, being a big fan of publications such as *The One Thing* by Gary Keller, and Cal Newport's *Deep Work*.[20] Theory rocks. But what I did not fully appreciate when trying to pare down a schedule for travel, was just how easy it is to end up seriously overloading on that very high-concentration task type, which requires the most focused attention. And that this is precisely the worst kind of 'get it done anywhere' kind of work.

A lot of less intense work I was able to get ahead on, delegate, outsource, delay or otherwise minimise, with an eye to not being available to work full-time, and having prolonged periods of travel. So that left me with a totteringly top-heavy to-do list of mission-critical things such as writing, research and pitching. Normally, these are things that I would carefully carve out time for in my working day and week, planning carefully to optimise factors such as lack of interruption, distraction potential and blood–caffeine levels, in order to accomplish them most effectively. Not things I would plan to cram in around errands and travel.

So, what happened? Well, it did all get done, although by the skin of my teeth in some cases, and not without far greater pressure than I prefer to create for myself. Also, by taking myself off in desperation to the nearest coffee shop – never my personal top choice for uninterrupted, high-concentration work, but sometimes the best choice is a compromise. We are fortunate enough to live in a time where we genuinely do have a lot of options about how and where we work, and travel time shines a spotlight on that.

However, this degree of open-endedness means paying greater attention, in the good old *Getting Things Done* paradigm, to the *context* of work.

When David Allen wrote the first edition of this seminal book back in 2001,[21] he was thinking of context in terms of access to technology: such as whether it is a good time to use the phone, see our email or have access to certain colleagues. Given that most of us nowadays have 24/7 access to

---

20   Gary Keller (2013) *The One Thing: The Surprisingly Simple Truth Behind Extraordinary Results,* John Murray Publishers; Cal Newport (2016) *Deep Work: Rules for Focused Success in a Distracted World,* Grand Central Publishing.

21   David Allen (2001) *Getting Things Done: The Art of Stress-free Productivity,* Penguin.

every possible task on our list and resources required, and because of this degree of accessibility, we may overlook the importance of the context dimension in everyday life.

When you are comfortably 'in your groove', you know what needs doing and can prioritise around your commitments and objectives successfully, depending on the importance and urgency of the task itself – without having to think about the kind of situation in which you would best carry it out. Recently, some Getting Things Done commentators such as Jeff Kirvin have talked about contexts more abstractly in terms of energy levels and concentration, and this makes a lot of sense.[22]

Had I reviewed my commitments prior to travel through a lens of context, I would have quickly realised that *I had seriously overstacked the generative, concentrated tasks which required complete attention*, and somehow planned to get them done during a week spent hot-desking at a relative's house or on train journeys: both perfectly good places to accomplish certain things, but far from ideal for this kind of work (at least they are for me – and self-knowledge is critical here).

Lessons for the future

Next year, I know that there are things I will do differently – in fact, I fully intend to take a proper holiday! But in terms of generally being away from whatever your workplace usually *looks like to you*, for example while travelling, I would suggest bearing in mind the following general learning points.

Prioritise

Even though it leaves you with the most important stuff inevitably, you still need to follow the Pareto Principle – the ruthless 80/20 rule – before you start in order to plan the rest of it. If you can identify the 20% of the tasks that bring the greatest value, and which most need your attention, focus on those first. The exact ratio might not apply perfectly, but it is easy to let less critical tasks crowd into your time when your day is more flexible.

---

22   Jeff Kirvin (2015) 'GTD contexts for working anywhere', 24 April. Available at: http://jeff.kirv.in/2015/04/gtd-contexts-for-working-anywhere/ http://jeff.kirv.in/2015/04/gtd-contexts-for-working-anywhere/

Don't take connectivity for granted
Even within the EU, think ahead to availability and cost of broadband. Also don't forget power: it is worth carrying a back-up power pack to juice up your phone battery – if you are using your phone as a hotspot, it can expire fast.

Upgrade your travel
Buy a better rail ticket or access to a private airport lounge, if it means decent connectivity and peace – because the cost benefit is obvious.

Use travelling time to catch up
When travelling, emphasise consumption rather than creation of information. Long journeys are great for reading, listening to podcasts, ripping through your Pocket queue (we discussed this nifty app in a recent podcast),[23] also for watching videos.

Bring the right tools
Take the right device with you to do the work you have planned. Just because you *can* theoretically do something on a device, does not necessarily make it the right choice. (Take it from someone who found herself doing copy-edits on a phone. On a train… Never again!)

Don't overschedule
Just because you happen to be in the same country as someone you don't always see, it does not mean that you have to go and meet them. Of course it might be the perfect thing to do for many reasons, but don't feel that you *have* to, if it means spending a day to accomplish a meeting that would have been an hour-long video call.

Watch your energy levels
Pay attention to your energy, especially if you are expending this on socialising for work or pleasure, possibly eating and sleeping more erratically.

---

23   Virtual Not Distant (2018b) 'WLP172: On the move', podcast, 31 May. Available at: www.virtualnotdistant.com/podcasts/wlp172-on-the-move

Communicate your needs

Make sure that family and friends understand. After nearly two decades, I have to say my travelling tribe are pretty well trained and on-message now: "Don't speak to Mummy while her headphones are on!" (and stay off the flakey borrowed broadband too, until she has finished her call).

Where you are the guest at others' homes, the people you visit might require more orientation about this. Try to stay cool when relatives turn out to have terrible broadband, after having assured you it is great! If they only use it for social media and games, it isn't their fault if you can't make a video call easily.

Don't let *all* of the admin accumulate

Try to streamline and stay on top of the faffy bits of admin, which you can potentially defer but are horrible when they mount up. Use little windows of time to line up social media (which really can be done on your phone), and scan and ditch receipts rather than stuffing them in a file to process at home. Your future self will be eternally grateful.

Home is where my work is

So, I am writing this now, back at my desk. In my ergonomic chair that is the right height, with my big paper planner open and all my different pens, with the reassurance that I could actually print something (although I rarely ever do). Then I could even shred it if I wanted to! Although I don't have to do so immediately, as it's not a shared or public area. In fact, I can leave all my stuff right here, overnight, as well.

While the summer adventures were fun, creative and energising in many ways, I am reminded that I love the freedom to be able to work from anywhere. But I usually love it most of all when that means right here, in my home office.

So much for the joining the digital nomads, Mac-backpacking and surfing of the physical kind. I know where I fit in.

Coda

So, what next?

While the subtitle of this book is 'inspiration for leaders of distributed teams', and we hope to have inspired you to define your next steps and actions – we also hope to have given you some specific guidance.

Perhaps the reflection questions in particular have helped you to zero in on specific areas which you already knew needed attention, or in other cases they might have surfaced new issues that you were not aware of at all. Either way, we hope to have nudged you closer towards resolving any areas of your remote leadership practice which could be improved.

We never said it was easy, though. Both of us run small businesses, and are in regular contact with enough managers to know that leading teams always brings plenty of challenges. However, we also know that the most joyful way of bringing a service or a product into the world is through collaboration.

If we have added a little bit of joy, or if we have helped you to remove a little bit of your pain, we would love to hear from you. And if you have found the book inspiring, we would love to stay in touch with you.

As well as our regular content made up of podcast episodes and articles (which you can find over at www.virtualnotdistant.com), we have created an email series to follow up *Thinking Remote*. This is aimed specifically at those with leadership responsibilities or inclinations, who are determined to take their remote collaboration capabilities to the next level. You can easily sign up to this over at: www.virtualnotdistant.com/thinking-remote.

And if you have got this far in the book, we are pretty sure you will be interested in our services and products, as well as our numerous blog posts and podcast episodes. On our website (www.virtualnotdistant.com) you will find all of this additional information and guidance, and a form to contact us directly with your feedback, suggestions and input.

Meanwhile, if you are ready to start a conversation about what you have learned with your colleagues or peers, use the leadership questions to start you off, or pick the article that you found most helpful and talk through it with them.

The future's bright, the future's flexible!

Pilar Orti and Maya Middlemiss

REFERENCES

Allen, David (2001) *Getting Things Done: The Art of Stress-free Productivity*, Penguin.

Duhigg, Charles (2016) *Smarter, Faster, Better: The Secrets of Being Productive*, William Heinemann.

Global Workplace Analytics (2015) 'Costs and benefits'. Available at: http://globalworkplaceanalytics.com/resources/costs-benefits

Google Re:Work (nd) 'Understand team effectiveness: Identify dynamics of effective teams'. Available at: https://rework.withgoogle.com/guides/understanding-team-effectiveness/steps/identify-dynamics-of-effective-teams/

Grant, Adam (2016) *Originals: How Non-conformists Change the World*, Virgin Digital.

Happy Melly (2017) 'Zappos lives its culture', podcast, 10 November. Available at: www.happymelly.com/zappos-lives-its-culture

Health and Safety Executive (2018) 'Work related stress depression or anxiety statistics in Great Britain, 2018, October. Available at: http://www.hse.gov.uk/statistics/causdis/stress.pdf?utm_source=govdelivery&utm_medium=email&utm_campaign=digest-8-nov-18&utm_term=report&utm_content=stress-stats

Keller, Gary (2013) *The One Thing: The Surprisingly Simple Truth Behind Extraordinary Results*, John Murray Publishers.

Kirvin, Jeff (2015) 'GTD contexts for working anywhere', 24 April. Available at: http://jeff.kirv.in/2015/04/gtd-contexts-for-working-anywhere/

Lydia M. (2015) 'How 15 minutes each week keeps our distributed team connected', Trello, 19 August. Available at: https://blog.trello.com/how-15-minutes-each-week-keeps-our-distributed-team-connected

Mann, Annamarie (2017) '3 Ways You Are Failing Your Remote Workers', Gallup, 1 August. Available at: www.gallup.com/opinion/gallup/214946/ways-failing-remote-workers.aspx

McChrystal, Stanley with Collins, Tantum, Silverman, David and Fussell, Chris (2015) *Team of Teams: New Rules of Engagement for a Complex World* (Kindle edition), Penguin.

Newport, Cal (2016) *Deep Work: Rules for Focused Success in a Distracted World*, Grand Central Publishing.

Scott, Kim (2017) *Radical Candor: How to Get What You Want by Saying What You Mean*, Macmillan.

Virtual Not Distant (2014) 'WP03: Informal communication in teams', podcast, 27 November. Available at: http://virtualnotdistant.com/informal-communication-in-teams/

Virtual Not Distant (2018a) 'WLP152 – Clarity and Transparency at MeetEdgar', podcast, 11 January. Available at: www.virtualnotdistant.com/podcasts/meet-edgar

Virtual Not Distant (2018b) 'WLP172: On the move', podcast, 31 May. Available at: https://www.virtualnotdistant.com/podcasts/wlp172-on-the-move

Vitality (2017) 'Long commutes costing firms a week's worth of staff productivity', 22 May. Available at: www.vitality.co.uk/media/long-commutes-costing-a-weeks-worth-of-productivity/

ACKNOWLEDGEMENTS

This book contains learning and experience from working with a range of clients and organisations, experimenting with different 'office-optional' ideas, and hearing personal stories. All the examples and anecdotes referenced are true stories with names and settings suitably changed to protect anonymity, and we are grateful to all the clients and collaborators who have allowed us to come with them on their varied journeys over the years.

Another great source of inspiration is the wonderful range of guests who have joined us on the *21st Century Work Life* podcast, whose generous sharing of their knowledge and ideas has taught us and our listeners so much. Reflecting such a diverse spread of experiences and activities, their creative thinking and input has helped us to refine our own theories and practice across the board.

Thanks must go to Manuel Barrio for being a guest in our online office while he was working on the book cover, Simon Heartshorne for the formatting of the book, and Lisa Cordaro for the great editing of our manuscript and going beyond the call of duty.

Finally, we are grateful to all the pioneers of remote working, flexible working, distributed working, smart working... Whatever you call it, however it looks to you, if you are courageous enough to try something different in your set-up, then you are shaping the future.

Keep at it, challenging assumptions and pushing boundaries – and don't forget to tell us how you get on.

ABOUT THE AUTHORS

Pilar Orti

After delivering leadership training face-to-face and facilitating team away-days, in 2010 Pilar started to look for non-location-specific opportunities to help people develop. Wanting to visit her parents in Madrid more often, and having met her future husband in Amsterdam, meant that limiting her work to her London base was no longer an option.

In 2013, she landed a freelance job with a training company, delivering accredited management and leadership qualifications online. There she began to ignite discussion on the company forum and growing its webinar programme. Far from finding the shift to the online space daunting, Pilar quickly adapted her ability to create a sense of purpose and unity to the online space, and in 2016 she set up *Virtual Not Distant*.

Pilar is fascinated by the opportunities that technology brings to make the world of work a better place. Seeing as we spend more than 70% of our waking time at work, what better way of helping make the world a better place?

As well as trying to improve the world of work, Pilar is a serial podcaster and loves to write (her current books and podcasts are available in online bookstores and podcast platforms). She is also an established voiceover artist: her credits include the voice of 'Xuli' in the CBeebies animation series *GoJetters*.

Maya Middlemiss

Following an early career in community development and voluntary sector training, Maya transitioned to home-based working at the turn of the millennium to found a market research fieldwork company. Finding few resources available at the time, she taught herself to develop and manage what turned out to be a fully-remote team, when it was still an innovative proposition – using a technology set-up which now sounds prehistoric.

As her team grew and technologies for location-independent working evolved, she took the opportunity to relocate to the Spanish Costa Blanca in 2009, seeking a healthier and happier lifestyle for her young family. She founded the fully-remote marketing communications agency BlockSparks in 2018, and hosts the *Crypto Confidence* podcast, as well as consulting and creating content for *Virtual Not Distant.*

Maya is passionate about the technologies and practices which enable people to communicate and work from wherever they are happiest, and the exciting times in which we live – being able to connect ideas, skills and potential from all over the planet to solve the world's problems and challenges.

73024456R00060